I0824646

ALSO BY ADA LIMÓN

Startlement

You Are Here

The Hurting Kind

The Carrying

Bright Dead Things

Sharks in the Rivers

This Big Fake World

Lucky Wreck

Children's Books

And, Too, the Fox, illustrated by Gaby D'Alessandro

In Praise of Mystery, illustrated by Peter Sís

AGAINST BREAKING

On the Power of Poetry

ADA LIMÓN

SCRIBNER

New York Amsterdam/Antwerp London
Toronto Sydney/Melbourne New Delhi

Scribner
An Imprint of Simon & Schuster, LLC
1230 Avenue of the Americas
New York, NY 10020

First Scribner hardcover edition April 2026

Interior design by Jaime Putorti
Map by Pete Sucheski
Illustrations: Library of Congress

Manufactured in the United States of America

1 3 5 7 9 10 8 6 4 2

Library of Congress Cataloging-in-Publication Data is available.

ISBN 978-1-6682-2472-4
ISBN 978-1-6682-2473-1 (ebook)

For Dr. Carla Hayden,
the fourteenth Librarian of Congress,
who is the best of us.

CONTENTS

Foreword • *xi*

Against Breaking: On the Power of Poetry • 3

Afterword • *51*

Sources and Permissions • *53*

A Note on the Author • *57*

FOREWORD

I served as the twenty-fourth Poet Laureate of the United States for three years. If you don't know what the Poet Laureate position is or what the Poet Laureate does, don't worry, you're not alone. Briefly, the Poet Laureate position was established in 1937, and the acting Laureate is tasked by the Librarian of Congress with promoting the reading and writing of poetry on a national scale.

This is not a role I applied for, nor was it something I expected. Instead, out of the blue, on a warm June Kentucky morning, I joined a mysterious virtual call that was set up by my representative and dear friend, Vaughan Fielder. Vaughan said she couldn't tell me what the call was regarding but, she added, "You might want to do your hair." On that video call, I was invited to serve as the Poet Laureate by the fourteenth Librarian of Congress, Dr. Carla Hayden. The small and welcoming staff that surrounded her on the call cheered and smiled when I accepted. And then, just like that, I was alone, in my small office, asking my beloved dog, Lily Bean, what on earth had just happened.

I met Vaughan for breakfast at our local meeting spot, where she handed me a giant bouquet of flowers and we wept and panicked in equal parts. I had planned to take some time off after my most recent book tour. I was going to rest. Instead, now I was to serve in the historic role that was occupied by poets I'd long thought of as personal heroes: Gwendolyn Brooks, Elizabeth Bishop, Robert Pinsky, Rita Dove, Robert Hass, Philip Levine, Natasha Trethewey, not to mention my immediate three predecessors, Juan Felipe Herrera, Tracy K. Smith, and Joy Harjo.

FOREWORD

In theory, there are only two obligations for this role: an opening reading at the Library of Congress and a closing lecture or conversation at the Library of Congress. What follows here is what I presented for my closing lecture on April 17, 2025. I was given a fifty-minute time limit, and I knew, despite wanting to say so much about the current state of the world, I wanted to do at least one thing: make a case for poetry.

During my three-year tenure, I threw my whole self into the work of it, into the joy of it, sometimes exhausting myself to depletion and numbness, and sometimes, thanks mostly to generous, hardworking collaborators—Vaughan Fielder and Rob Casper, to name a few—making big public projects that I count as some of my proudest accomplishments.

I routinely found myself in surreal situations. I celebrated the National Student Poets in the State Dining Room at the White House. I traveled to Mexico City as part of Un Fandango por la Lectura, a celebration of music, dance, and poetry hosted by Dr. Beatriz Gutiérrez Müller, wife of then president of Mexico Andrés Manuel López Obrador—with special guest Dr. Jill Biden, the First Lady of the United States. I read poems for the First Lady of France, Brigitte Macron, and Dr. Jill Biden during their visit to the Planet Word Museum in Washington, DC. I wrote a poem for the National Climate Assessment. I wrote a poem for the National Gallery of Art. I wrote a poem to honor the thirtieth anniversary of the Violence Against Women Act. I wrote a poem that was engraved, in my own handwriting, on a spacecraft called the *Europa Clipper* and watched that spacecraft as it was launched into space at NASA's Kennedy Space Center in Florida. Perhaps *surreal* isn't a strong enough word?

And together with the National Park Service, the Library of Congress, the Poetry Society of America, and Milkweed Editions, we launched my signature project: *You Are Here*. As part of *You Are Here: Poetry in*

Parks, we put poetry installations on picnic tables in national parks around the country, including Cape Cod National Seashore, Mount Rainier National Park, Redwood National and State Parks, Great Smoky Mountains National Park, Cuyahoga Valley National Park, Saguaro National Park, and Everglades National Park. In addition to those installations, we created an anthology of new nature poems called *You Are Here: Poetry in the Natural World*.

We stood under giant trees and surrendered some part of ourselves back to the land. We stood in the desert and watched saguaros at sunset transform into exclamation points all over the darkening hills. We shouted when we saw new bright birds at the edges of fields, and delighted when we encountered baby elk following their mothers into the understory near the Pacific Ocean. We met with tribal elders and indigenous communities. We asked permission. We listened. We met with underrepresented groups that wanted to feel welcomed into their local park wilderness. We met with people who loved nature and people who were frightened of it. We met with people who loved poetry and people who were frightened of it.

During all those trips, all those planning meetings, and those meticulously orchestrated events and readings, what always amazed me was how many people were doing the good work out in the real world. All over this country there are stewards of the land working to save and preserve whatever they can. There are librarians who are eagerly adding poetry books to their expansive collections. There are people organizing reading groups and poetry workshops in rural communities and urban centers. Educators working overtime to inspire young people to write about this planet. Everywhere I went, I was reminded of what generosity does for the spirit. I came back from each trip not depleted but fueled up and inspired. I fell even deeper in love with poetry.

On April 17, 2025, when I walked on the stage in the Coolidge Auditorium in the Jefferson Building of the Library of Congress, I walked onstage holding everyone I'd met and worked with in my heart. Our nation was changing in dangerous ways that we were just beginning to witness. We knew what was coming. I wore a green suit for my friends in the National Park Service and for all the stewards of the earth. I wore earrings from Mexico for my Mexican immigrant grandfather and for all immigrants.

I wrote this for a roomful of people at a storied library that was coined "the people's library" by Dr. Carla Hayden. I wrote this for our beloved Dr. Hayden, who first invited me to serve as Laureate and who was unceremoniously removed from her post just three weeks after I gave this speech.

The evening was charged; the room was packed. I could barely breathe until the faces in the room encouraged me to do so. In this printed volume, I hope you will hear the crowd breathing together, and I hope you will feel as connected as we did in that moment. I hope you feel invited into the room, the large room we all must create together, the room where we all must work hard to save what matters.

AGAINST BREAKING

AGAINST BREAKING: ON THE POWER OF POETRY

Truth be told, any time I begin to write anything these days, my whole life flashes before my eyes. I ask myself, *Do I want to break something, or do I want to mend something? Or simply try to carve out a small place to breathe?* I want, and have always wanted, only to make something true. And what is true these days? And how does one know? The truth feels slippery and mysterious. Even the words *the truth* feel like something of a marketing gimmick, a slogan that's selling some impossible outcome.

When clarity is hard to come by, when language has morphed into a tool for confusion, I put my faith in

poetry. Then, if I'm lucky, if I'm quiet enough, lines of poems I love start to move through me. They come to me as if through a necessary beckoning.

The lines of poetry that come to me first when I am at the beginning of anything are from Yeats: "I must lie down where all the ladders start / In the foul rag and bone shop of the heart." And so, yes, let me begin there, "in the foul rag and bone shop of the heart." Then, I think, instead of at the bottom of a well, shouldn't we begin in celebration? And Lucille Clifton comes to me: "won't you celebrate with me / what I have shaped into / a kind of life?" Or Robert Hass's poem "Faint Music," which starts with the lines "Maybe you need to write a poem about grace. // When everything broken is broken, / and everything dead is dead." Yes, maybe it is time to write a poem about grace. Or do we begin in urgent chaos, as the poet H. D. did when she began her poem "Sheltered Garden" from 1915: "I have had enough. / I gasp for breath"?

You see, if we are lucky enough to live a life in poetry, we are never alone—we are never alone because everyone who has ever written is with us. The great book of all of us is being written together, with everyone who has already written—in every human language, and perhaps even in language that we don't recognize as language—and everyone who will someday write. And sometimes we even place our own words there, tenderly, eagerly, to remain for others to find.

It can seem at times like a selfish act: to write poetry, to devote a life to poetry, something only a solipsistic navel-gazer might do. I understand that impulse to roll your eyes at poets and poetry. I remember a friend in graduate school who used to come to readings and poke fun at the poets. "Oh," he'd say, pretending to clutch a poem in his hands, "my blanket is so sensitive." We'd laugh and laugh because he wasn't wrong. Our blankets were sensitive and we wanted to tell you about them. When so much is needed, desperately and urgently, in the world, how can one make an argument for poetry?

Would it be an exaggeration to say that poetry saves lives? Maybe. Maybe not. During my tenure as Poet Laureate, I came to realize that not only are people hungry for poetry, language, and connection, but that for so many people around the world, it already serves as a much-needed lifeline. It can be how we situate ourselves in the world, see ourselves reflected, or recognize our own suffering and our own joy. I've traveled now to almost every state in the union, and it seems to me that there is no place where poetry isn't alive and thriving. Sometimes it might only be a handful of people, a few outliers who share poems in the library or at a local dive bar on the edge of town, and sometimes it's a large and rowdy crowd, but poetry lives in all communities.

When I first began to serve in the role of Poet Laureate, I thought my job was to bring poetry to the people, but that's not what happened. The

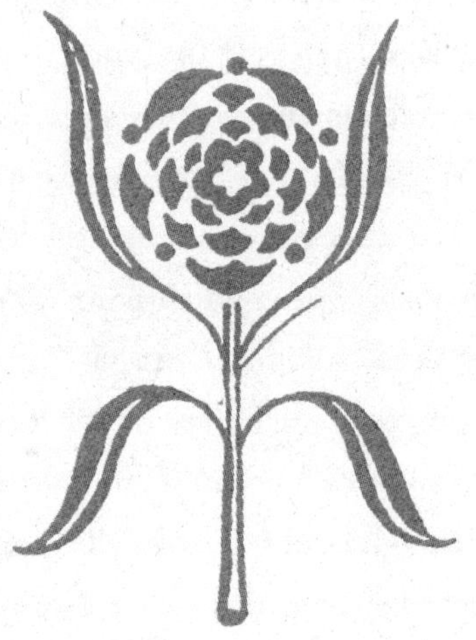

offering was not central to my experience; instead, it was the receiving. In the last three years of my tenure, I had the great good fortune to listen to people tell me what poetry means to them. One woman, her eyes blue and earnest, told me that her grandfather started memorizing poetry after his son died in war. He memorized poems so he could keep them in his mind while he stood in line, while he waited. It kept his mind busy so it didn't go into the dark places. She said, leaning into me close at a reception, "Before he died, he gave each one of his grandchildren one of those poems he'd memorized so we'd always have it as protection."

Another woman, who was born in Mexico, stood in line at a bookstore, and told me that she had trouble holding on to both Spanish and English in her head, so she began to write original poems in Spanish and then translate them into English as a way of witnessing the world in two languages. Back and forth, she'd translate her own words. Eventually, she could not just understand the language but hear its music.

Deep in the California desert where a town manifested out of nowhere, out of tumbleweeds and red rock outcroppings, a young student said, "I read this book every day when I was in the hospital for over two weeks. When I was too sick to read it, my mom would read it to me." It goes on like this, stories of people carrying poems in their back pockets until they were so worn, creased, the paper soft with wear, they couldn't be read anymore. You can find poems in hospitals or at funerals, on bathroom walls. Sometimes, years of silence are broken when someone begins to write a few words on a page. Maybe poetry *does* save lives.

I woke up one morning recently with some lines by Stanley Kunitz in my mind. It was from his poem "The Testing-Tree": "In a murderous time / the heart breaks and breaks / and lives by breaking." Saying it helped me get out of bed is no exaggeration. I rose and washed my face and looked in the mirror and was made braver by poetry. My heart is living by breaking, but my heart is living. And how many people quote Mary Oliver when they need her? For me it's these two lines in particular: "I don't know exactly what a prayer is. / I do know how to pay attention." Or when I'm stuck in the middle of something difficult, some immovable obstacle in front of me, I conjure up Jean Valentine's poem "Door in the Mountain." I stare out a window, or at a challenge in my mind, and say her last lines: "Door in the mountain / let me in."

This is the secret power of poetry. Little engines of sound urging us on, telling us we are not alone, because we can't be; we are connected to the readers and writers of poetry. Recently, at a reading in the Deep South, an older man came up to me, in a neatly pressed white shirt, telling me he was embarrassed to say that he only wrote poetry privately, poems he'd never share. What a gift to be able to

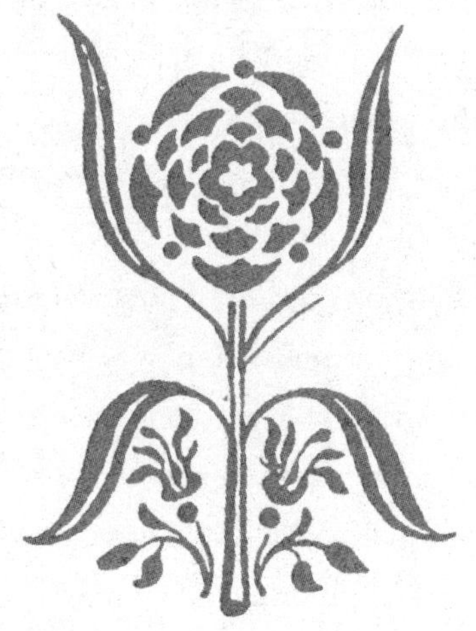

witness his confession and to assure him that many people make the same confession. I remember, as he spoke, I stared at the coffee cup someone had placed next to the book table. It said, "Handle with care." Yes, handle all of us with care, we who are open to the world of poems.

It gives me great joy to know people are writing secret poems. And if you are one of those people, I want you to keep going. Even if you never hand it to another person. There is power in making private poems. Aren't we all walking around with some unsaid pain, or some uncelebrated wonder? Aren't we all trying to find a place for our rage and despair?

Is any poem ever a failure because it goes unpublished or unshared? No, because didn't it make you pay attention, the act of writing? Didn't you, even briefly, feel as if you inhabited the world? Didn't it, for a moment, make you feel connected to language? Didn't you find a container for your heart?

It is, perhaps, easier to explain what writing and reading a poem can do to a person than it is to explain what a poem actually is. "What is a poem?" This is a dreaded question that's so difficult to answer. Ask a poet and we immediately say infuriating things like, "What is a soul? What does the color green mean?" This is one of my favorite things about poetry: You can put all the poets in the world together in one room, and instead of one definition of a poem, you'd have many.

This is another one of poetry's secret powers. It makes room for how utterly different we all are. It has no interest in sameness, flatness, homogeneity, and yet it is deeply human and can be, at times, universal. How is this possible?

I once asked a neuroscientist, Heather Berlin, what surprised her most about her work and research on the brain. She responded, "That anyone gets along at all or that anyone can be in a relationship with anyone else, because our brains are so different." I've never forgotten that conversation, and it struck me as so revealing.

If we are built so differently, why on earth are we ever trying to be the same? We aren't supposed to be the same, we aren't supposed to write the same, we aren't supposed to make the same art, or have the same beliefs, or love the same things, or love the same way, or worship the same way, or speak the same way. That's, well, that's what machines do.

We are not machines. It's no surprise to me that with the exponentially rapid rise of artificial intelligence, we are reexamining our relationship with technology. And in my mind, we are putting too much faith in it. I have deep concerns and anger about AI, and its use of our poems, words, and personal literature. As importantly, I worry about its use of water, one of our most precious resources. As a poet, I wonder: Why would we ever want AI to make art for us? Isn't that one of the singular joys we get for ourselves? But perhaps it's no surprise

that people want to see if AI can write a poem. Why? In my opinion, it's because we want to know if AI has a soul. We want to see if what we created is indeed alive. And poetry is a way of testing for humanity, individuality.

But if our brains are all so different, how do we ever expect to relate to one another or understand each other? To empathize? How do we, as Heather Berlin asked, ever enter into relationships with anyone? This is where poetry comes in. If you've ever wondered what someone was thinking or how they remembered a certain event or how images unfolded in their minds, and what the inside of their thought patterns might look like . . . then you've wondered what their poems might look like. You've wanted to open their secret selves like one might split a rock to find a geode inside, and that geode, that sparkling surprise—that's poetry.

Listen, let me interrupt myself here and admit that there are days that I do not want to read a poem. And there are certainly days that I do not want to write a poem. Why is that? Because there are days when I don't want to feel. Or rather, I only want to feel safe and soft things. Poetry does the work of opening us up to our feelings, and it's not surprising that it can often make people cry, even those of us who very much wish not to cry. It's my belief that this is why adults often think poetry is for children: not because they want it to be taught to children but because they think children have more of an emotional range. I'd argue this is exactly why poetry needs to be more integrated into the lives of adults. We need to be reminded that we are, at the end of the day, deep feelers. And if we can admit our feelings, then we might be able to move in the world with more equanimity and courage.

I'm not saying that feeling is easy. I am saying that to make art is to admit that we have complex feelings and thoughts that cannot be summed up.

Poets must surrender to the mess of the world and the mess of themselves. For me, it's as if a poem is always being made. It is being made now. We are making it. You and I, reader and writer, listener and speaker, my past self who wrote this, my present self who reads this, my future self who is wondering what the hell I was talking about in the first place.

While there are ways to teach poetry, mostly we learn by reading and writing, writing and reading, and then going out into the terrifying world and feeling so much that those feelings threaten to collapse us onto the concrete, facedown and forever ruined by human cruelty or even love. And then something happens; there's some moment when you think, a little gravel on your cheek, "This suffering might make for a good poem." Or, "This wonder might make for a good poem."

You might not even be thinking of a poem; rather, you might think of the words themselves. "Is

this concrete or cement that I'm lying facedown on, and what, really, is the difference?" "Oh," you might begin to think, "it's that the *c* sounds are different. A hard *c* in one and a soft *c* in the other like in music. The hard *c* in *concrete*, like *cave* or *crash* or *catastrophic*, compared to the soft *c* in *cement*, like the *sea* itself or like *supple* or *simmer*." And of course, even if at this point you've entirely forgotten to interrogate the real material difference between concrete and cement, you have determined that they are entirely different because they sound different. This is how a poem is made. In the cement mixer of the soul.

And your cement mixer is different from mine. And isn't that marvelous? When you read another person's poem, you are entering their music and their syntax, and because of the line breaks, commas, caesuras, and stanzas, you're entering their breath. It's oddly intimate. We can inhabit each other's lives just by reading a poem aloud. It's this intimacy that prevents us from being alone.

At a time when loneliness is being called an epidemic and division seems as basic to our daily lives as breathing, how could you not want an art form that allows for a type of connection, a connection that is on a human frequency, not a social media platform? The algorithm of the body and soul.

And while this might not seem like a secret power of poetry, the fact that it is very difficult, if not impossible, to monetize poetry allows for poetry to remain subversive. Poetry has the benefit of being outside economic systems.

Is that a fancy way of saying that poetry doesn't make money? Yes. But it's more than that: Poetry is meant to be free, it's meant to be given, it's meant to travel one poem at a time, like pollen from a tree floating through the air to make more trees. Poems travel that same way. And because of that, they remain sacred, unbothered by trappings of the usual oppressive systems.

I think of Gregory Orr's poem that reads:

How lucky we are
That you can't sell
A poem, that it has
No value. Might
As well
Give it away.

That poem you love,
That saved your life,
Wasn't it given to you?

. . . .

The secret power of poetry also fuels the public power of poetry. The way poetry affects the individual also helps move the collective. Perhaps, in dire and dangerous times like these, all poetry can do is remind us where courage comes from. And if that's the case, maybe that's enough.

Who doesn't need a little nudge these days to keep going, or to be braver? Sometimes that bravery is private and individual, something to get you through this day to the next or this hour to the next. But sometimes poetry can also help us gather strength collectively.

I still remember sitting on the subway after September 11 and reading the first issue of *The New Yorker* that was published after the towers fell. It had a black cover, nothing but the space where life once was, and I read Adam Zagajewski's poem "Try to Praise the Mutilated World." I know this isn't true, but in my mind, everyone on the L train was reading it together, all at once, flipping to the page where the poem ends:

You've seen the refugees heading nowhere,
you've heard the executioners sing joyfully.
You should praise the mutilated world.
Remember the moments when we were together
in a white room and the curtain fluttered.
Return in thought to the concert where music flared.

You gathered acorns in the park in autumn
and leaves eddied over the earth's scars.
Praise the mutilated world
and the gray feather a thrush lost,
and the gentle light that strays and vanishes
and returns.

For weeks afterward, that poem was passed from hand to hand, read and shared. That poem was the only thing that made sense. When all the rhetoric of war and nationalism and violence was blotting out the sun, this poem saved me. I said it to myself like a mantra: "Try to praise the mutilated world, praise, praise, praise."

It wasn't just the poem itself or the instructions it insisted upon, but the way it reminded me that language had power. And it could have power for good.

We need a secular sacred language, something that is galvanizing without certainty, that gathers us

without gathering under one ruler—but under the connection that we all have to the human spirit, to each other, to the earth. Listen, friends, I am tired of violence, I am tired of hatred, I am tired of the antihero being made into a hero! I am tired, I am tired, I am tired. But you know what isn't tired? Poetry.

Poetry is just getting started. It's just coming out of the dust and rubble and beginning to learn the intricate song of this time. And we need it. Is it an intellectual endeavor? Sure. Is it a bodily excavation of memory and haunt? Yes.

Is there rage? Yes. Is there room for wonder? Yes.

Langston Hughes wrote a poem that has been shared quite a bit recently, and I keep returning to it:

Tired

I am so tired of waiting,
Aren't you,
For the world to become good
And beautiful and kind?
Let us take a knife
And cut the world in two—
And see what worms are eating
At the rind.

The poem might be called "Tired," but it's also a call to action. It's a poem that's getting ready for what's next.

Poetry in the public realm has the power to form connections, foster courage, and refuel us for what's coming. If I can make an argument for poetry that exists in the darkened corners, in desk drawers, back pockets, might I add that there are times when poetry should be dragged back into the light?

When I was writing this piece, I asked a few non-poet friends what themes were coming up for them and what, if anything, was giving them hope. One friend was particularly despondent, and he said he was finding very little hope these days. But then, after a moment of silence during which I wondered what devastating news he would share, he sent me a poem. Turns out hope was at his disposal in the form of a poem. Language itself offers a message of resilience.

When I created my signature project as Poet Laureate, *You Are Here*, I wanted to make room for more public poems. Because of my own connection to nature and the need for all of us to protect and preserve our planet, we worked with the National Park Service to put poems throughout the different regions of the national parks. The Library of Congress team, and the incredible park rangers and National Park Service staff members—all of us—believed that poems might help us do one simple thing: Pay Closer Attention.

An accidental encounter with a poem can bring you back into the world, can remind you that you are in the world, part of it. I remember riding the subway in New York and noticing one of the poems in the *Poetry in Motion* series. It was called "Return," by Robert Creeley, and it ends with the lines, "Enough for now to be here, and / To know my door is one of these." I read it and watched others read it. And it did feel like enough for now, just to be here, hurtling through the dark tunnels together.

Public poems and chance encounters have the power to shift us but also to commemorate something that matters. Over my last year serving in this role as Poet Laureate, I've watched as people from all over the country have come to see legacy poems unveiled at our beautiful, necessary national parks. They sat around the poetic installations and read them aloud together. It might not seem earth-shattering or monumental, but language in these public spaces matters.

In one of the most recognized public spaces, we can find what is arguably the most public poem in this country. At the base of the Statue of Liberty, millions of people have read "The New Colossus" by Emma Lazarus, a poem that's been memorized again and again with its lines that echo through the entire country:

Not like the brazen giant of Greek fame,
With conquering limbs astride from land to land;
Here at our sea-washed, sunset gates shall stand
A mighty woman with a torch, whose flame
Is the imprisoned lightning, and her name
Mother of Exiles. From her beacon-hand
Glows world-wide welcome; her mild eyes command
The air-bridged harbor that twin cities frame.
"Keep, ancient lands, your storied pomp!" cries she
With silent lips. "Give me your tired, your poor,
Your huddled masses yearning to breathe free,
The wretched refuse of your teeming shore.

Send these, the homeless, tempest-tost to me,
I lift my lamp beside the golden door!"

While Emma Lazarus died at thirty-eight, her poem lives on, defining the most generous version of the United States, a version that is barely recognizable now. This poem changed the meaning of the Statue of Liberty forever, and it is nearly impossible to think of Lady Liberty, her torch thrust into the air, without thinking of the sonnet that was engraved on its base in 1903.

. . . .

The word that I keep coming back to is *belonging*. Public poetry can give us a sense of belonging. While I toured the national parks, meeting the park rangers, the stewards of our beloved natural spaces, it felt like placing poems in these lands was a way of offering something back to the places that hold us, the places that are larger than any of us. It felt as

if we were all coming together to demonstrate that we belonged to this earth, not that it belonged to us. And for a brief moment, maybe, it felt as if we belonged to each other as well.

In Cuyahoga Valley National Park, the sun was hot. My dress had ripped completely up the back, and we rushed back to the hotel so I could change into a backup suit I'd luckily packed at the last minute just in case. The suit was hot onstage in the summer Ohio heat. I was tired and feeling a little bruised by the world. But I had a moment when I thought, "This is what we are supposed to be doing, gathering for the sake of nature, under this enormous tree, reading poetry for each other, and doing what Adam Zagajewski told us to do, after September 11: praise, praise, praise."

A huge crowd had come out to hear poetry and celebrate their park. There were picnic blankets and folding chairs. Kids running on the lawn. It seemed to me no one there was immune to the ongoing suffering of the world, the very real violence that all too often defines humanity. No one there wanted to escape the realities of our world, but instead we wanted to say, "This too exists. This place, this grass, this wildland with its clear river that once caught on fire—this can also be a part of our human experience." And while watching them all before I took the stage, Ross Gay's poem "Sorrow Is Not My Name" came back to me, including the passage:

there are, on this planet alone, something like two
million naturally occurring sweet things,
some with names so generous as to kick
the steel from my knees: agave, persimmon,
stick ball, the purple okra I bought for two bucks
at the market. Think of that.

I've argued for most of my life that poetry is powerful in part because it exists in the questions and holds no answers. It's the opposite of a polemic, or a prescription; instead, it's an interrogation of the world and one's place within it. That said, even though it doesn't hold answers, perhaps it *is* an answer.

When my maternal grandfather died, my grandmother, his wife of seventy-six years, leaned toward me, right after the funeral, and said, "Now, teach me poetry." And I think about that daily. Poetry responds to things that are too large to be said, when the feeling is too big. Even as I write this in prose, I find myself resisting the sentences. The need for clarity of thought. It's not that I don't want to be clear; it's that I trust the mystery so much more. The images, the way in which each individual story returns to me all at once as I say these words.

Audre Lorde once wrote, "If I didn't define myself for myself, I would be crunched into other people's fantasies for me and eaten alive." Poetry can help prevent us from being eaten alive, because if

we write it, we are allowed to reframe the narrative, recenter the truth, and reimagine a different type of future. If we are readers of poetry, we can search for the poems that allow us to feel not just seen but beheld. The right poem can make us recommit to the world.

At this very moment, we need to gather strength and resilience and compassion in any way that we can. Perhaps poetry, for you, is the secret place where you get to be as free and as safe as you can; perhaps you can make that blank page a place where you can lay down everything you need to lay down. Maybe it's where you go to get stronger; maybe it's where you go to become softer. But know there is a place that you can make on the page that no one controls but you. In that, right there, is a mighty power.

As I was scrolling through social media recently, looking for anything that could give me a little sense of connection, I ran across an influencer who told people that they had permission to live "a big life," but I'd like to add that the small life needs to be recognized here too. We don't just change overnight; courage doesn't come from a depleted place. We plant seeds; we take care of our families, of each other; we bring food to a neighbor, or clean out litter from the creek bed; we listen to our favorite song while driving; we read a poem. A big life requires a small life. They do not exist without each other.

While poetry can be unifying and energizing for crowds and in the public arena, it is also a natural caretaker of the small life. We cannot rise to our full power if we are not paying attention to what we give our attention to. Poetry can be our lens for discovering how we can find our own worth, the individual gift we can offer. It's easy to be overwhelmed by how much needs to be fixed, how much work there is to be done. It's also easy to shrug and think a poem can do nothing against the powerful chaos that's building all around us. That's when I think of this Emily Dickinson poem:

If I Can Stop One Heart from Breaking

If I can stop one heart from breaking,
I shall not live in vain;
If I can ease one life the aching,
Or cool one pain,
Or help one fainting robin
Unto his nest again,
I shall not live in vain.

Sometimes, all poetry offers me is possibility. When the world says things are impossible, poetry says, Is that true? What if the new story starts here? What if the center is not where you think it is? What if those that steward and protect are gathering now as we speak and what rises next is a whole new epic beginning?

No one knows how this ends.

As with beginnings, lines of poetry come to me when I'm ending something too, like these lines from Alberto Ríos's poem "A House Called Tomorrow":

Look back only for as long as you must,
Then go forward into the history you will make.

Be good, then better. Write books. Cure disease.
Make us proud. Make yourself proud.

And those who came before you? When you hear thunder,
Hear it as their applause.

If everything we know about the world is true, then we will all die someday. This is a fact that most poets are intimately aware of. Why does poetry matter, you ask? Poets respond, Because we're all going to die. What do we do with that? We pay close attention to the world because paying attention is a way of saying thank you, a way of loving.

Recently, I wrote a poem about the ancient woods in the Kootenai National Forest in Montana. This forest is in grave danger due to the threat of a proposed logging project. As a thank-you for the poem, one of the stewards of this land sent me a package full of aromatic branches and detritus, pine needles and small larch pine cones, from the forest floor. The package smelled like the entirety of the earth. He included a note that said, "I am so grateful." I thought, "This is a poem": a handful of earth sent to a friend, with a thank-you bound to its core.

I want to do that for you, reader, listener: I want to send you a box of the earth, and I want you to hear my thank-you.

It has been one of the greatest honors of my life to serve as the twenty-fourth Poet Laureate of the United States, and I want to leave you with this: When you want to create a safe space to stand in, to breathe in, to gather courage, to find your hope again, to find your strength again, you can stand in poetry. It's my belief that poetry is something we are all making together, and it belongs to everyone around this planet. And it does not believe in nations, or borders, or cruelty, or power for power's sake, or wars, or violence, or causing harm; poetry wants us to be our free and best selves, open to wonder and open to making a life that matters—both big and small. As poet June Jordan once wrote so brilliantly, "We are the ones we have been waiting for." And we are.

But if I cannot explain to you what poetry is, how can I convince you to love it, or tell you that it matters? There is also some part of me that wants to say, if you can't understand why poetry matters, that's okay. If you don't love poetry, that's okay, I release you; be well, be free, be exquisitely removed from this conversation.

And yet, and yet! I want everyone to know this kind of magic. The poetic life offers a different relationship with the world, one that is trembling with feeling and music and attention. It can change you and hold you and reunite you with your own humanity.

It could be that I'm the wrong person to convince anyone of anything. I say hello to crows as if they'll say hello back, and sometimes they do. I shout at trains to see if I can match their howling and point at the moon because, you know, it's the moon. But if you feel the need to trust language again, to remember that language could have power, could hold multiple truths, then you need poetry. If you need to be reminded of what makes us human, tender, brave, flawed, and worthy of love, then you need poetry.

Listen, I am not saying you have to love every poem I love, or love the poetry that I write. But please love something. In fact, that's what poetry—secret or shared—can give us: a chance to write toward what we love, to name it, to sing our sorrow so it does not break us, to bear witness to this moment in time, to become stronger, to retrain our minds toward what's good in this world, to what's good in us. Maybe all poems remind us of this? Like a hidden refrain etched in every line, in every stanza, something silently echoing: You have to love.

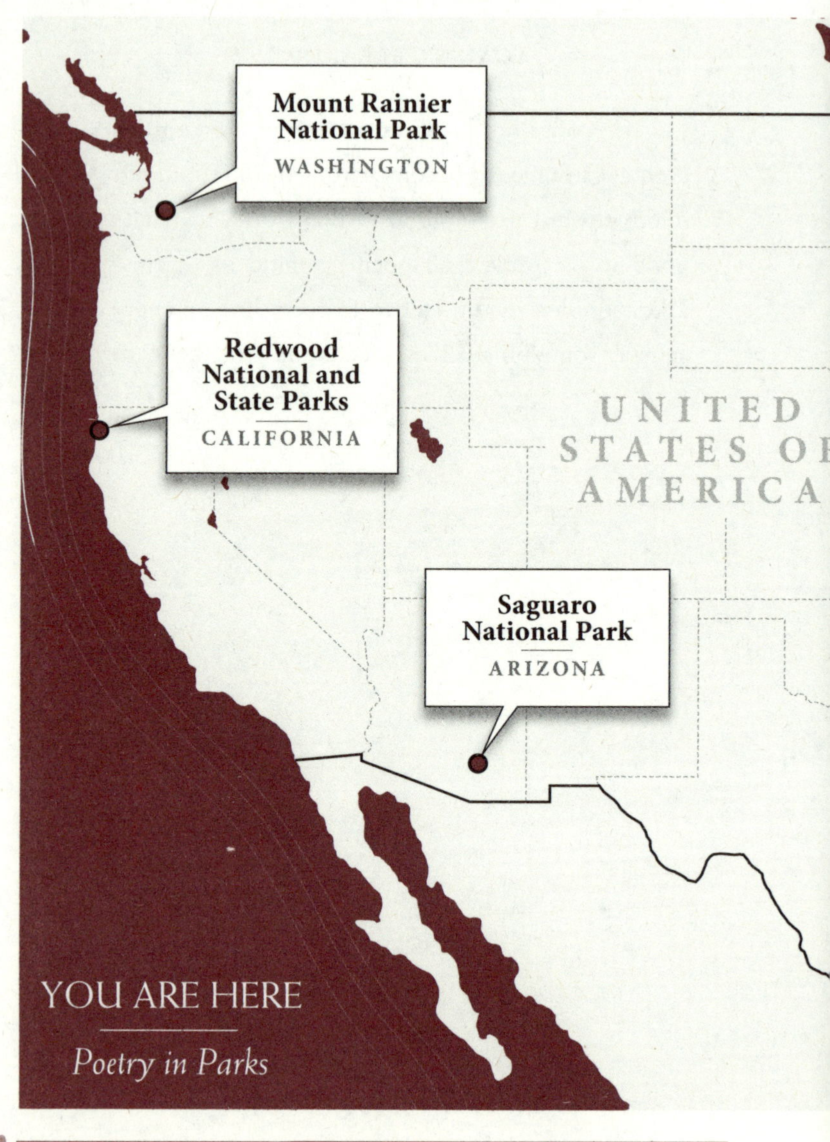
Mount Rainier National Park
WASHINGTON
Redwood National and State Parks
CALIFORNIA
UNITED STATES OF AMERICA
Saguaro National Park
ARIZONA
YOU ARE HERE
Poetry in Parks

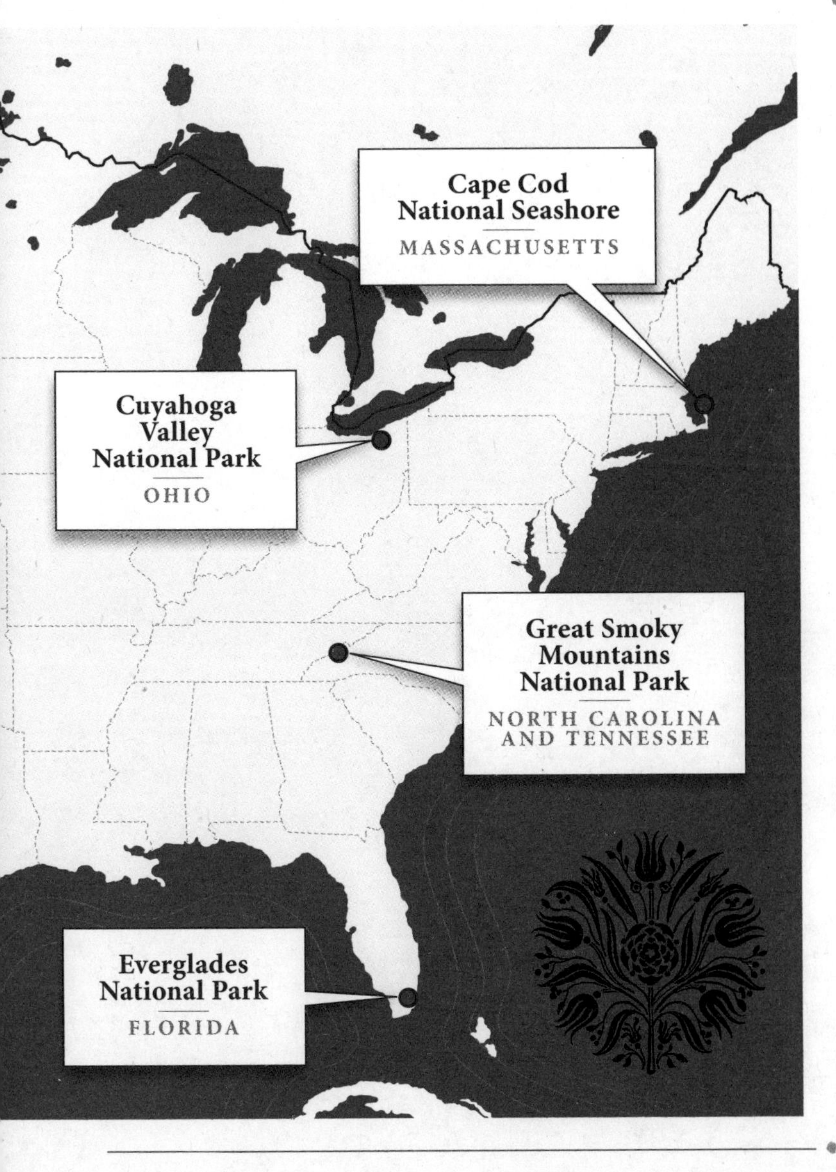
Cape Cod
National Seashore
MASSACHUSETTS
Cuyahoga
Valley
National Park
OHIO
Great Smoky
Mountains
National Park
NORTH CAROLINA
AND TENNESSEE
Everglades
National Park
FLORIDA

AFTERWORD

Thankfully, the *You Are Here* project still thrives, and you can visit the poetic installations on accessible picnic tables in parks around the country.

Mary Oliver's poem "Can You Imagine?" is in the Cape Cod National Seashore (Massachusetts), at the trailhead of Beech Forest Trail.

A. R. Ammons's poem "Uppermost" is in Mount Rainier National Park (Washington), outside the Henry M. Jackson Memorial Visitor Center.

Francisco X. Alarcón's poem "Never Alone" is in Redwood National and State Parks (California), at the Redwood Creek Overlook.

Jean Valentine's poem "The valley" is in Cuyahoga Valley National Park (Ohio), at the Ledges Trailhead.

Lucille Clifton's poem "the earth is a living thing" is in Great Smoky Mountains National Park (North Carolina and Tennessee), at the Appalachian Highlands Science Learning Center.

Ofelia Zepeda's poem "Na:nko Ma:s Cewagĭ / Cloud Song" is in Saguaro National Park (Arizona), at the Mica View Picnic Area.

June Jordan's poem "Ecology" is in Everglades National Park (Florida), at the Ernest F. Coe Visitor Center.

SOURCES AND PERMISSIONS

The following poems are quoted in *Against Breaking*, with thanks to the poets:

"The Circus Animals' Desertion" by William Butler Yeats

"won't you celebrate with me" by Lucille Clifton

"Faint Music" by Robert Hass

"Sheltered Garden" by H. D.

"The Testing-Tree" by Stanley Kunitz

SOURCES AND PERMISSIONS

"The Summer Day" by Mary Oliver

"Door in the Mountain" by Jean Valentine

"How lucky we are" by Gregory Orr

"Try to Praise the Mutilated World" by Adam Zagajewski, translated by Clare Cavanagh

"Tired" by Langston Hughes

"Return" by Robert Creeley

"The New Colossus" by Emma Lazarus

"Sorrow Is Not My Name" by Ross Gay

"If I Can Stop One Heart from Breaking" by Emily Dickinson

"A House Called Tomorrow" by Alberto Ríos

Permissions

Gregory Orr, "How lucky we are" from *Concerning the Book That Is the Body of the Beloved*. Copyright © 2005 by Gregory Orr. Reprinted with the permission of The Permissions Company, LLC on behalf of Copper Canyon Press, coppercanyon press.org.

Excerpt from "Try to Praise the Mutilated World" *Without End: New and Selected Poems* by Adam Zagajewski, translated by several translators. Copyright © 2002 by Adam Zagajewski. Translation copyright © 2002 by Farrar, Straus and Giroux. Reprinted by permission of Farrar, Straus and Giroux.

A NOTE ON THE AUTHOR

Ada Limón is the author of seven books of poetry, including *Startlement: New and Selected Poems*; *The Hurting Kind*, which was a finalist for the Griffin Poetry Prize; *The Carrying*, which won the National Book Critics Circle Award and was a finalist for the PEN/Jean Stein Book Award; and *Bright Dead Things*, which was named a finalist for the National Book Award, the National Book Critics Circle Award, and the Kingsley Tufts Poetry Award. Limón is the recipient of a MacArthur Fellowship and a Guggenheim Fellowship and was named a 2024 *Time* Woman of the Year. She is the author of two picture books, *And, Too, the Fox* and *In Praise of Mystery*, and was the editor of the anthology *You Are Here: Poetry in the Natural World*. She served as the twenty-fourth Poet Laureate of the United States.